Rorschach Art Too

Rorschach Art Too

poems

Stephen Gibson
Donald Justice Prize Winner

Story Line Press | Pasadena, CA

Rorschach Art Too

ISBN 978-1-58654-368-6 (tradepaper)
978-1-58654-004-3 (casebound)

The National Endowment for the Arts, the Los Angeles County Arts Commission, the Ahmanson Foundation, the Dwight Stuart Youth Fund, the Max Factor Family Foundation, the Pasadena Tournament of Roses Foundation, the Pasadena Arts & Culture Commission and the City of Pasadena Cultural Affairs Division, the City of Los Angeles Department of Cultural Affairs, the Audrey & Sydney Irmas Charitable Foundation, the Kinder Morgan Foundation, the Meta & George Rosenberg Foundation, the Allergan Foundation, the Riordan Foundation, Amazon Literary Partnership, and the Mara W. Breech Foundation partially support Red Hen Press.

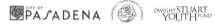

Second Edition
Published by Story Line Press
an imprint of Red Hen Press
www.redhen.org

Acknowledgments

Grateful acknowledgments are made to the editors of the following magazines in which these poems, or earlier versions of them, first appeared:

Alimentum: "Bread"
Bryant Literary Review: "George Segal's *The Butcher Shop*"
Court Green: "Triolet on My Wife Looking at a Sandwich-board Menu in Ischia"
The Journal (as The Ohio Journal): "Mushroom Gathering"
Measure: "On Seeing Fra Angelico's *The Annunciation*" and "Villanelle for Skeletons"
nd[re]view: "Noir"
Notre Dame Review: "*Susanna and the Elders*"
Plume: "Infidel Ghazal for a Church Skeleton"
Poetry: "The Peat-Cutters"
Quiddity: "Bones"
River Styx: "*Morphinomaniac*"
Salamander: "On a Tapestry Copy of Guido Reni's *Slaughter of the Innocents*"
Sou'wester: "Margins 2"
The Southern Review: "*The Flayed Ox*" and "Hamper"
The Texas Review: "Address to the Tollund Man" and "Plague Year, Marseilles, 1347" (the latter reprinted in Measure)
The Third Wind: "The Peat Bog Finds"
Western Humanities Review: "The Body in the Bog"

Thank you to Kim Bridgford and to Pat Valdata, and to everyone at West Chester University's Donald Justice Prize, for helping to bring out this collection, and a special thanks to Dick Davis for selecting the manuscript.

For my brother Tim and my lifetime friend Ed Falco, my love and gratitude.

Finally, thank you Mark and Kate.

Contents

Always for Clo, Kyla, and Joe

I

Past/Present

Trompe L'Oeil in a Benedictine Church

—Melk, Austria, 2013

Behind the railing ringing the cupola,
we're told, one of the two brother artists
has himself, elbows and all, leaning over—
if you look there, he's looking down at us,
the guide says, and we follow his finger—
and, sure enough, he's there as saints recess
upward behind him, foreshortened figures
giving us the illusion of added distance—

and then we're told that all of it is false:
not only him or the shrinking figures
heaven-bound, but the cupola itself—
a flat ceiling was the artist's canvas—
which may be why he smiles leaning over:
what we think we see may be something else.

The Café at the Corner of ....

—Vienna, 2013

Maybe it's the whole history thing
that's bummed for me this place's ambience
rather than piqued it—Vienna's alliance
of rationalists met here offering
an alternative to mysticism and cult-thinking
then rampant between wars (a sentence
including "between wars" shouldn't make sense,
but does) because while Freud ordered something
at one of these marble-topped tables (accidents
happen—I could be at his favorite ordering
strudel and coffee), Stalin did his thing
here, as did, of course, that failed art-student
Adolf (info all-inclusive with our trip-
advisor). I don't care what he ordered or tipped.

Zeitgeist at the Café Central

—Vienna, 2013

After I order an espresso and the strudel
I read about the famous who also ate here
(it's why I came—it's like a second menu):
Freud, Trotsky, that watercolorist Hitler;

arrived in England, with jaw cancer, of course,
Freud didn't have a whole helluva lot
of time after he left (the vanilla sauce
comes in its own tiny earthenware pot—
it's real cream, not the milk-flavored Crisco
like you find in half the joints in London);

Trotsky fled all the way to Mexico
thinking he could get away from Stalin
(no cheap after-dinner mint or toothpick):
he was wrong—Ramon got him with an icepick.

Das Unbehagen in der Kultur
("The Uneasiness in Culture") at the Café Central

—Vienna, 2013

When Freud dined here I wonder if he stared
at women's breasts, like I'm doing
(the one behind my wife might as well bare
them because her blouse is so sheer, clothing
in her case is really a fetishist thing
meant to arouse, not to have someone not stare),
but as I was just a moment ago thinking,
I wonder if Freud, with all of mankind's cares
and neuroses dumped into his lap, could bring
himself—sitting here like I'm sitting here—
not just to watch a beautiful babe walking
to her table, but sitting down at it, to wonder
(like Henry does in Berryman's *Dream Songs*)
what wonders she's sitting on, with a thong.

Ghost Dessert Menu at the Café Central

—Vienna, 2013

It's not offered on this one, but like some
poltergeist menu in my head, I see written
(as history-buff, not historian), at München,
(Munich) the watercolorist (as heavy-handed
with Chamberlain as with Daladier), demanded
around-the-clock negotiations with no breaks
(not possible—and there was a luncheon
after, at which Mussolini, the buffoon, grins
at everyone—it's recorded in eight-millimeter
and can be viewed on YouTube), and when done,
because of the possible Jewish origins of Sacher
torte, AH gorged himself on whipped cream cakes
(after being delivered Sudeten Czechoslovakia),
and strudel with his initials in powdered-sugar.

Noir

Sometimes what you're not looking for, you get.
In January of 06, at the Metropolitan Museum,
I stood in a hallway looking at these photos: one
was of this lesbian bar scene in Paris, the 1930s,
with this silky-looking femme holding a cigarette,
blowing smoke rings at this guy who had her knee
in one hand and his thick arm around her neck,
clueless about what was to happen to him.

You see, sitting across the table was the femme's
butch lover—large—in pinstriped suit and tie,
whose face told it all: she was taking it all in,
and didn't like what she was seeing, not one bit.
The photo caption told the rest: she cut the guy
open like a melon and did hard time for it.

The Peat-Cutters

They live as their fathers lived and those before them.
In thick boots made to last for years
they go out on mornings and harvest fuel
from fields too sodden for hands to farm
and spade the peat mass into bricks, which leave
wide, rectangular holes behind, the size of carts.

Somehow these fields seem never diminished.
Though worked in the same manner for centuries
hawthorn and beech and dog's mercury
have lain down with other vegetable matter
forming fresh layers decaying near the top,
which, in time, under pressure, are driven downward.

And like their Iron Age ancestors who worked
these sites (and who turn up everywhere
a spade goes down—the bog has properties
which preserve the skin), the peat-cutters
still go about their lives, uncomplaining of tourists:
in the isolated villages, girls marry young;
the men are as good as their word, and remember wrong.

The Body in the Bog

(*Grauballe Man*)

It was always there, needing to be found,
a corpse buried in a field of peat,
just in walking distance past the house,
put there by someone, not yourself, who thought
a thing kept down so long can't hold its breath.

Of course, it did. But who would think the dead
would keep? Meat spoils in a day and milk
soon clots; what sunlight ripens on a limb
eventually decays. But in this fen
the corpse remained intact, even its organs

as fresh as if your wife had watered them
in secret, hidden inside the flower pots
she keeps beside the bed. (They face the window
she faces out, closing themselves at night.)
Air escaped when a shovel opened up its chest.

It was planted, then, to bring forth grain:
They buried the corpse for seed so their women
(who worshipped metal hammered into rings)
would swell like melons under skin. Their skirts
have also been preserved in the bogland.

Address to the Tollund Man

The body is that of a young woman, perhaps
a sacrificial offering to a fertility deity.
Her corpse, found well preserved beneath the
layers of an ancient Danish peat-working, lies
close by to that of Tollund Man.

Consort of a goddess? Or can't they guess?
They see the necklace that was hung on you.
A man would cut a pig with more finesse

and sympathy. Your fault was, more or less,
nothing; that is, being a nothing who
would be her consort. Or couldn't you guess?

(You lowed like a calf and made a mess
of things—exactly what they thought you'd do.
A man would cut a pig with more finesse.)

Myself? They hung on me *adulteress*,
a tag a woman knows is false or true
and also meaningless. Or couldn't they guess

that what a woman is, is, not more or less—
they shaved my head and had a blindfold too.
(Who needs a mirror for one's last hairdo?)
A man would cut a pig with more finesse.

Long Island Noir

Someone is killing women and dumping their bodies
on Long Island, behind sand dunes, in thicketed,
remote, inaccessible areas a person normally tries

to avoid, but police keep finding them. The body lies
naked, head first in brush, as if it washed up dead,
but someone is killing these women, dumping bodies

in what has become a morgue awaiting new entries
each time an earlier one leaves to be documented.
It's a remote, inaccessible area a girl normally tries

never to go to—but these young escorts advertise
they will satisfy whatever a man dreams up in bed.
For one, it's killing women and dumping their bodies.

The youngest was nineteen—she had stars in her eyes,
studied acting, went out on night calls, her roommate said.
Broadway is a remote, inaccessible area, but a girl tries.

The junkie older sister of another said the press told lies
about them turning tricks—crying, she turned her head.
It wasn't Jane Doe someone killed, dumping her body.

Each one had a name, an address, and life stories
the rest of us only care about because they're dead.
Someone is killing women and dumping their bodies
in remote, inaccessible areas so easily, he hardly tries.

Infidel Ghazal for a Church Skeleton

—Vienna, 2013

The casement seems as hard as the jewels they set in you for eyes.
Someone thought emeralds were a safe bet after you died.

(Unlike yours, I found a five-and-ten emerald-jeweled butterfly
pinned to an old sweater of my mom's in the closet after she died.)

They laid out your skeleton as if you were lying on your side
writing with a feather, but Death was the architect when you died.

(Brueghel saw your ilk in monk's black robe, with scythe, ride
a white horse through plague-swept Utrecht as thousands died;

Jews poisoned wells; witches were convicted and then tried—
Mother Church as a plague ravaged city and hamlet and millions died.)

The past as present, death after life—they both in you reside,
not as *memento mori*, but as Hollywood set—and the actor died.

Sonnet for a Skeleton

—Vienna, 2013

It isn't enough: the jeweled silver vestments,
some weighing twenty pounds, some more,
or the silver-threaded shoes, or gold crozier
once placed in your palm and the fingers bent
around it, or the cappello that you once wore
in life to block sun burning into pavement
on walks, or the falda, with its regiment
of train-bearers holding it off the floor
(why is that missing from the glass casement
under the altar?); it's not enough—the mitre,
the finger-bones in their arrangement, the feather
writing instrument that someone bent
a finger-joint around and dabbed with adhesive—
it isn't enough: death is death—you don't live.

Envoi to a Skeleton

—Melk, Austria, 2013

This skeleton in its aboveground crypt
(part base of a side-chapel altar)
is also decorated with tulips,
like a skirt around it in construction paper,
which anonymous schoolchildren finger-
painted and signed, their permission slip
for this dead self not to have to linger
among schoolchildren, but to begin his trip
to where his parents are (among the tulips
are painted male and female stick figures:
blank faces—jots or smears with fingertips),
each individual panel signed in a corner
by a child who one day in the future
will be given this send-off given a stranger.

Villanelle for Skeletons

—Vienna, 2013

I'm sitting in a cathedral with a few
minutes to kill—Clemens will not avert
his gaze, knowing I'm waiting, like you

for something more. In the next pew
I overhear a woman say her feet hurt
and that also makes me think of you,

on yours all day in "sensible" shoes,
same white blouse, same black skirt—
they hung in the closet waiting for you

(bagged for Goodwill, they hadn't a clue);
they ended up on someone needing a shirt—
like Clemens, who makes me think of you,

you, underground, and him in plain-view
but in the same place, just different dirt,
which waits for me as it waited for you

(no matter the date, the bill overdue)—
propped on an elbow, posing like a flirt,
Clemens watches me thinking of you,
grinning, knowing I'm waiting, like you.

II

Brief Histories

Plague Year, Marseilles, 1347

"Not fish are eaten, nor even spice": Gui,
who sat between two fires to melt the fat
and dissipate the humours, for whom ammoniac
and moonwort were prescribed (though fleas
were spots of pepper on his sausage legs),
appears in guttering light, his calf's moon-
face, seen in the depression of a spoon,
flares up momentarily with the ashes, begs
Our Lady's grace for this leveling
and shrinking of options; whose life was milk
to his family who now are wretched wights
because an illness left physicians nodding;
who woke, only to rasp into her silk
handkerchief, and was dead within two nights.

Mushroom Gathering

an entire family found poisoned in 15th century France
—from a dining-guide article about wild mushrooms

Because only the poisonous Death Caps tarnished silver
and they had no silver, neither bowl nor sliver

of bread to sop up soup; because no servant's trained hog
would root out truffles for them and accept an acorn;

because they'd eaten every "household deer" (field mice)
their dog could corner, squeaking their whiskers at straw

in their meal sack—he burned his children's bedding
and ordered that they all go out into the country.

And because the delicate morel was rarer than butter,
rarer than Chardonnay to sauté them in—rare whether

whole-chopped-or-sliced to grace a salad; and because
no "fairy ring" of mushrooms appeared at morning to grace

their table, he sent his daughters out to help their mother,
to ask Christ Jesu's blessing and to fill their aprons,

and they ate.

Bread

In the infomercial, the paid audience shouts out
the pitchman's tag line, all of them shilling for bread.

In the Great Famine of 1315, some Paris bakers
are charged for using pig shit as filling in their bread.

Don't look at me, man. Didn't I say don't look at me?
It don't matter, killing is killing—show me the bread.

When Chang and Eng wanted out of their contract
with him, P. T. Barnum wasn't willing—bread is bread.

Gangrene, hallucinations, spontaneous abortions: in medieval
Europe, thousands die; ergotoxicosis; something in the bread.

Margins 2

After publishing his theory on the evolution
of favored species through natural selection,
Darwin often suffered long spells of illness.

Nothing could heal him: the rests
from work, his wife preparing water cures,
these could not heal him. The fiction
of a safe existence lived indoors.

His thoughts were illness. A mind
spent on barnacles and orchids,
crustaceans, and the eccentricities
of beaks. Details proved the death

of species. And after the deluge
of publication, there were more bodies
than could be counted. On country walks
he witnessed the usual slaughter:

life lived at the expense of life;
nothing fittest, and such prodigious waste.
He dreamed himself hunted through Europe's cities
where swarms of insects bred in swamps.

Ophelia
—Viking Danube Cruise

She talks about her teen daughter's death
over breakfast, and says yes to more coffee
too, as our Philippine waiter serves me
and then goes over to her—she holds her breath
as he leans over to pour, signaling with wavy
fingers, enough. She thought it an accidental death
at first, but it wasn't—she sucks in her breath
as if a doctor has told her to count to three
while he examines her, then let it out; she does.
The table goes round with spoken apologies
for her loss, or silence over what once was
an enjoyable breakfast. This isn't Surrey,
or Millais painting some Pre-Raphaelite model
he'll later sleep with. The girl, fourteen, took pills.

Noir Sestina

When I was a kid growing up in the Bronx,
the Sunday *Daily News* ran crime stories
always in the centerfold of the paper,
after the international news in the front
and always before the sports news in back,
which gave the previous night's box scores

and were more important than the scores
of dead in Indochina. This was the Bronx.
Who was fighting who wouldn't bring back
Whitey Ford into the rotation—that story
meant the Yanks were in trouble; the front
collapsing at Dien Bien Phu was newspaper

ink, a bunch of words on page 3 of the paper
that didn't even rate a photo (unlike a score
being settled, with the mob guy dead in front
of a barber shop somewhere in the Bronx,
which didn't give the full details in the story,
just a cutline under the photo, then back

to the real story about the boss going back
for an indeterminate stretch). The newspaper
let you know what was important. The story
was front page? News. A Yankee score
in the ninth inning—headlines in the Bronx.
The Viet Minh in Indochina? A commie front

being directed from Beijing with Mao out front
but it was really Moscow (the story doubling back
to hearings uncovering cells even in the Bronx).
One story, though, stayed with me from the paper.
It wasn't international news; it wasn't a box score.
It was in the *Daily News* centerfold, a crime story.

A young woman was strangled. That's the story.
Her killer, walking between buildings, saw out front
on a clothesline a pair of underwear among a score
of wet panties on other clotheslines. So he went back.
The killer claimed he never knew the woman. The paper
told how he climbed the fire escape. This was the Bronx.

A crime story. Looking back, I understand randomness.
Out front, he saw a pair of sexy underwear, the paper said,
out of scores of panties on other clotheslines in the Bronx.

'60s Hudson Valley School of Painting Noir

She is awake, eyes open, looking up through the ice.
The skaters on the pond at first don't see her there.
As if caught by wind, her scarf flies over her head.
In snow, crows leave behind their cuneiform script.
They caw from bare tree branches, the only sound.
Taken from in front of her house, she disappears.

Through glass, a red pickup stops, then disappears.
The realization has the suddenness of a slip on ice—
her daughter is not outside and there is no sound.
One moment she saw her, and then she wasn't there.
She will say this over and over as if reciting a script.
Police will ask her again, and she will hold her head.

She looked out through the window, and, in her head,
unconsciously, she knew—a toy in the yard disappears,
you instantly sense its absence. Each day has its script,
unique, familiar, but it can upend you like a slip on ice.
She was in the kitchen, looking out, didn't see her there.
The snow-filled yard was empty; there wasn't a sound.

The tire chains made a whirring, slapping sound—
which made her gaze out of the window, her head
preoccupied with soup in a pot about to boil there,
but as one thought makes another thought disappear
she forgot the soup, hearing tire chains spinning on ice,
a different sound, something not part of the day's script.

A red pickup patched with Bondo wasn't in the script.
She looked out the window when she heard the sound.
The rear tires had chains on them, spinning on the ice.
Then the chains caught and the pickup bucked ahead.
She watched it go behind the trees until it disappeared.
Only then she realized that her daughter wasn't there.

Felt in the Hudson Valley School of Painting, there
is a reverence for the natural landscape, unscripted
and unmarred by the material world, which disappears
for the viewer, to be replaced by the sights and sounds
of stillness arrived at like some mantra in the head
in painting after painting of snowy hills, snowy fields, ice-

frozen ponds, where there is no human and no sound.
But scripts left by crows have meaning only in our heads.
Birds make tracks. A murdered girl appeared under ice.

Hamper

Whether it was made in Bangladesh or Pakistan or India
you can bet women sat on dirt floors to weave this hamper.

Highly shellacked, darkly stained, with twin brass fasteners:
in Pier I Imports, you said it was a widow's empty hamper.

Do you remember the time you screamed in the bathroom
because our son was playing hide-and-seek in the hamper?

(I can still see you standing forever under the shower-head
after your mom's funeral, your panties on top of the hamper.)

This shared life of ours—my plain, practical Hanes briefs,
your Victoria's Secret secrets—some of you, me, in a hamper.

The Peat Bog Finds

"Above all level off the threshing floor. . .
And bind it well with chalk to kill the weeds
And keep the crumbling dust from opening chinks:
For then all sorts of plagues will pester you. . ."
—Virgil's *Georgics*

". . .most desires end up in stinking ponds. . ."
—Auden

Whatever men thought nested in these fens
There is a totem carving found near here
Set among scrub birch, and ash, and poplar
As if it had rooted. It bears the rough-hewn
Strokes of someone carving dead wood
Into something bearded, whose eyes,
Lidless on the face, survey these fields
And project a sense of expectation. (The eyes
Are growth rings knotted into tumors.)
Whatever this was, its truncated torso
Was meant to suggest, perhaps, the swoop
And rising arc of scythes just before
The shocks are bundled; or maybe
A crescent-moon was meant, the fertility
Of harvest somehow linked to phases—
Where, and what to seed, how deep to cover,
When to walk barefoot so the tubers ripen.
It is difficult to know with certainty.
In any event, when clouds blacken, brackish
As fen water, and the wind whips
The tree limbs into frenzies, there is the illusion
Seen through this flailing that the mouth
Of this gleaner gapes and gashes;
That the torso flaps like a bird wing....

What can be said about a raised corpse laid
At your doorstep? "The ground sank around it
And exposed a hand." "The men had just gone out
This morning to load the barrows." "There was rain
All this week." "During the last century
A priest reburied one in consecrated ground."
"They had no names."

                         But are characterized
By properties peculiar to the peat
That keeps the bodies fresh and the organs
So moist you'd think the dead were kept
As sweetbreads or as sausage. Bloated with grain,
Colons never emptied, the intestines preserve
An infinite variety of foodstuffs—
Chiefly grasses—made into a gruel
And fed to them. So what can be said?

That earth did not dissolve these corpses,
That years of rich decay and other cover
Deepened and compacted and covered over,
Until the dead, once hidden, left no impression,
Neither as something unknown pushing to surface
Like a disturbed root in a field or garden
Heaving off grave-dirt where the bulbs are buried
(Which then necessitates removal, here
And elsewhere; wholesale carnage clear to bottom);
Nor as a slight articulation of the surface
Which the eye dismisses but examines later—
Thinking the field it saw was only level—
In the center of which, however, disturbing
As the slightest bulge in a ceiling's plaster,
Was a rain eroded, rounded formation,

Perhaps a barrow.... That this is cut away now
By the curious, who sink their probes
Into the mire like skillful doctors
Feeling for a tumor, difficult to locate—
And you, awake, not knowing what is being
Excised, turned over, or left entire, but
Compelled to answer—these objections I've thought,
But no matter. Once a god, Anubis himself—
A man below, the face a jackal—
Directed the fingers of his priest-embalmers
Whose twisted rods and slender curving hooks
Worked in blindness toward the ethmoid bone
To scoop the brain out through a nostril.
Later, that one who stood outside the tent,
Who'd be assailed with execrations when
The task was done, entered with a black stone
To eviscerate the corpse the god had marked
(Performed also upon cats, thought sacred).
The organs—lungs, stomach, liver, intestines—
Were cleansed and scented; deposited into jars.
Only the heart remained inside the body,
Thought to be the seat of intellect and feeling.
These corpses surface, however, some
With the startled eyes of fish; others with grimaces....

Millennia separate this corpse from us
(Cf. pollen analysis of the strata), yet if
The soul could peer inside this grave-ditch
It would cringe, stiffen into cardboard,
And hold its breath. It would not be, that viewed
This close, death seemed horrible or grisly,
Although it is this—for the man's face,

Pushed into peat, appears to be grazing
(When they lift him, the stringy turf so fills
His mouth that clods hang like a feedbag).
Nor would this death, being remote, cure
Our interest; neither the convolutions
Within the dented brainpan, nor the colon's
Contents will do this. The soul, if anything
(To continue the suggestion) would cringe,
Scenting its own detection. It would be
Found out. Perhaps a body/soul analogy
Is useful here. This is the illusion:
A hand moves a compass to describe
A circle and gives void a dimension.
This is the soul we confuse with its absence.
It is like the snake, that primordial
Omphalos, you, having an appetite
May have dreamt of often, and forgotten:
Swallowing its tail-end, it contracted
Into a pinpoint, and disappeared....

So many surface. Whom to examine?
The one whose spots, appearing on the skin,
Were only thought an insect's bites, merely
A blemish? Whose inflammations—
Now walnut size, erupting through the groin
And from under armpits—are to be treated
(This is the diagnosis) with spells, lotions,
Or poultices, either until the blackness
Drains, or god works a cure. (Both, he dies.)
In the lifespan of a rat's migrating flea
There are how many turns, miscalculations—
This coat too far, that straw will burn—

Blind alleys leading to a single exit?
Or in the troubled thoughts of someone
Who thought this was dog flesh (dogs turn up
In these peat bogs), who damages a face
We recognize? This is another, dating
From the plague years....

                              Maybe a different tack
Is needed, something to hold this narrative
Together before it unravels—like the coarse
Cloth sacks their women wore, cinched
At the waist and serving a double function.
Every necessity goes into them,
Real or imagined.... Think of an insect:
The nymph straddles a reed or piling
Set in water, where her drowned reflection,
Either a blur or in focus (it doesn't matter)
Seems wholly unconscious. Sensible only
To her own darkness, her sides twitch like the walls
Of a cocoon, or perhaps like nerve ends
Beneath an eyelid. (Imagine a party,
Your eyes open beneath the blindfold.
This is her darkness.) Now in a moment
Something explodes along the brain-stem,
Sending this message: the skin along the back
Splits, and a dun-colored imago,
Almost transparent, steps out of its coffin—
Which may, still rigidly attached
To the plant stem, appear to be waiting.
There are moments, as the death-grip fastens
And the ghost emerges, when the one appears
To regard the other as if it would linger.
There is an instant before separation

When both seem conscious. (This, of course,
The credulous believe, for who, fearing
Annihilation at the final tremor,
Would be abandoned? As for lingering,
The frenzied *entrechats* of this insect
Result from oozings inside the husk, thick
As a glue pot.) This is the adulting
Of a damselfly, whose singular function
Is ingenuous in nature, and proscriptive:
As an exact casting of its mold—
A nymph with wings, but reduced in size—
The adult's external mouthparts will not function.
These are fused, whether closed or open,
Their joints frozen as if they'd been soldered.
Thus deprived, its life becomes one long ménage
Of random copulations, lasting one month.
Now, to these women.

                        The way the living clothe
Their dead is always instructive. P.V. Glob found,
For example, the splayed carcass beneath
A blanket had been a drowning. Branches,
Forming a cage or basket, kept her from floating.
She was a stand-in for a goddess.
There are others: men cut to the neckbone
Who spilled like bladders (perhaps
A regenerative symbol, much like a fountain?);
There are adulteresses and accidents,
Old and recent (these fens are treacherous);
This is my understanding, though I've not seen one.

III

Rorschach Art

George Segal's *The Butcher Shop*

Take a plaster body cast of a dumpy
butcher, set her across from a plaster customer
(the meat cleaver poised above a chicken's
neck), and you'll understand what sickens
about Segal's sculpture. For all of their
homey homespun appearance, her Zen-
like stoicism as she holds the cleaver
above the bird, the neck stretched out to her
on the block—this is not about peace, or tension
from all directions bringing about stasis.
This is about guillotine blade and carcass,
and the cruelly anonymous exchanges
of ordinary life. There's nothing peaceful
about Humpty-Dumpty sitting on a wall.

Susanna and the Elders

—Not Lorenzo Lotto or the Uffizi, but Florence

Her ripped fishnet pantyhose hung
on a wall hook to the left of the toilet
in the after-hours bar, which the manager let
him use once the punk high-school-young
hostess changed, leaving her unstrung
black boots trailing their laces on the wet
tile, her pink mini & black leather jacket
hung next to magic-markered tongues
licking clits in sheetrock. Beside the water
tank (minus wood-handle on the pull chain)
& on the cracked mirror, undreamt of orgies
(promised in nail-polish), offered daughters,
wives, sons (followed by cell numbers), as he
watched soapsuds popping at the drain.

On Seeing Fra Angelico's *The Annunciation*

—Metropolitan Museum of Art, January 2006

She dreamt it was a finch trapped in her apartment
that wandered in and then, somehow, couldn't
find its way out.

                  She watched everywhere it went:
as it disappeared into the draperies and sent
shivers down them, as it flew into the window,
fluttered, and then fell back onto the bureau

and then, it seemed, looked at her the way pets do
when the pricked vein registers and they look at you
with that look when it's the end on the vet's table
(if what you see in their eyes is there, being animal),

but that was how it looked to her, and in the dream
it didn't fly off, but among hairbrush and jar of cream
moisturizer and lipstick, it died—and she, helpless,

heard herself awaken to, *I don't want this, I don't want this...*

Morphinomaniac

("The Morphine Addict")

After a lithograph by Eugene Grasset, 1897

There's nothing she won't do, this wild-
looking piece of chicken, needing to get high.
When she hikes her skirt, take a wild
guess (as she injects her thigh)
at how old she is. She'll lie,

tell you X (for it to be filed
away till later, when you try to reconcile
yourself with what you buy:
her, the spike in the muscle, her vial
on the table). There's nothing she won't do

to please, down on her knees—as a child
her petite pouch satisfied dozens. (Try
not to think about that; focus on the lie.)
        There's nothing she won't do.

On a Tapestry Copy of Guido Reni's
Slaughter of the Innocents
—Vatican Museum

In this huge copy of Guido Reni's
Slaughter of the Innocents, men of power
turn their backs on death and tourists;
soldiers avert their eyes as throats are slit
in much the same way goats have theirs, or
veal calves, when they're yanked from teats
and left to drain so that the meat is tender.
I'm in Rome, it's a hot July day in 2004,
and in my left hand is a Vatican Museum ticket.
I've been waiting in line for hours for one door
to open—into the Sistine Chapel. *The floor*
of the gallery is Travertine marble, I fake it
to a pretty Aussie girl beside me. I ignore
thinking about Iraq when I stare up at the tapestry.

Triolet on My Wife Looking at a
Sandwich-board Menu in Ischia

Who can resist a pizza Margherita
with a glass of wine, both for seven euro?
When we were young, she'd eat half of hers.
Who can resist a pizza Margherita?
I'd ask her. She'd smile, put a hand on my shoulder
and leave me all of that crust and tomato.
Who can resist a pizza Margherita
with a glass of wine, both for seven euro?

Improvisation on Two Photos by Diane Arbus

The girl cuts herself, cuts the tops of her thighs
high up so that the skirt she's wearing hides
what she does. She does it to feel something,
anything, and sometimes she does feel—a sting.

She cuts high up, but the skirt she's wearing hides
what the razor does—a razor not at her wrists.
She'll do anything to feel something, and not die.
It's all there is, but it's enough when nothing else is.

The thigh cuts help keep the razor from her wrists.
It's one of her father's Wilkinson Sword Blades.
It's all there is, but enough when nothing else is.
Like that skinny boy in the park with his toy grenade.

It's one of her father's used Wilkinson Sword Blades
that she found in the wastebasket in the bathroom.
Like that skinny boy in the park with his toy grenade
she immediately understood its potential for doom.

The razor found in the wastebasket in the bathroom
was used to shave a face and not to cut open wrists,
but the actual always has the potential for doom
like Arbus opening a vein after she downed barbiturates.

The Flayed Ox
—Rembrandt

If his aim was to be a realist, to show
us what muscle and bone and sinew
look like and how they attach to each
other, then the milkmaid looking on,

touching muscle and bone and sinew
is meant to be us, staring at its cavernous
opening, all of us, like milkmaids looking
at something recently alive, now hanging.

Or is the ox us—us staring at cavernous
barreled ribs, sinew, and marbled muscle;
us recognizing something alive, now hanging,
as us; us as it hanging from a barn's joist,

half-barreled ribs, sinew, marbled muscle.
Staring into its dark, cavernous interior, does
she see us, us hanging from a barn's joist
tied with ropes by its nether hocks, splayed,

us staring into a darker, cavernous interior?
We see her as us in another way, as the ox is,
tied with thick ropes by its hocks and splayed:
she posed, modeled for the artist in the flesh,

posed herself in another way, as the ox is
posed, captured in a moment as it was, not is.
The artist's model posed for him in the flesh.
That's her, as she once was, staring at an ox

posed, its captured moment as it is, not was,
her captured moment also as it is—and was.
Rembrandt's model posed; she once had flesh,
muscle, bones and bowels and sexual organs—

that's her, captured in a moment as she was
before it became another moment, then none.
Nothing—muscle, bones, bowels, sexual organs.
Nothing. It, her, in a moment became nothing,

but before it became nothing, it had moments
that looked like each other and were attached
to each other like muscle, bone, and sinew are—
inseparable and real; like ox and milkmaid, show.

IV

In Memoriam

Bones

—Saint Anthony's Basilica, Padua

1.
I've seen chicken bones like them next to my car
when I've gone home from work: a tiny one
was in a filigreed gold on glass case kept far

enough back behind a marble railing
(but close enough so that you could still
see that it was the tiny bone of something—

maybe even human—though you couldn't tell
for sure, at least I couldn't, because most bones
in churches look like bones from Pollo Tropical

or KFC, only not in wrappers, which someone
discarded because they're too lazy
to walk ten feet to drop them into a garbage can).

Anyway, I had been in line waiting to see
the relics of the saint this beautiful cathedral
was built for when all around me appeared these

young nuns, I think from the Philippines, girls
really, but who were already wearing habits—
and that got me to wondering about how well

we make our choices, and why we do. I mean, it
must mean something for these girls to give up sex,
to "marry" Christ, and to put on the habit,

when all of it, I think, is a hoax, especially relics.

2.
I've seen photos of Raymond Dart
holding the skull of Taung Child in his
open palm: the domed part

of the skull that housed the braincase
was as small as a baseball.
Dart named it *Australopithecus*

africanus. In Venice, I stood before a wall
filled with relics from the floor
up to the ceiling—knuckles,

skull fragments, bone splinters
(some looking like they'd been chewed for their marrow).
You could stand so close that you saw

through the lead-trimmed windows
of the glass cases the smallest bones' vacuum
openings. Even in the tiniest bones, the hollows

were so distinct, you could count them.
And maybe that's what the guy
next to me was doing. I watched him

tapping away at his Blackberry,
making people have to go around him to view
the rest of the reliquaries,

or maybe he was texting someone—you
weren't supposed to use cell phones in the cathedral,
which had one old guard, and he was into
collecting wet umbrellas, warning people not to fall.

3.
Dying isn't a hoax—a couple of weeks before
my mother died of liver cancer,
she came to Florida

to visit my wife and me and her grandkids, Kyla
and Joe. My kids couldn't believe
what they saw—

grandma's dying, they both said to me.
They said this in private,
pulling me aside as if I couldn't see

the obvious—and they were right.
It's not that I refused to see the obvious—
she was dying—it's that I never considered it

a fact that could happen to her. I made us
oatmeal each morning, and one morning
when my wife took the kids to the bus

I watched my mom's empty hand bring
an invisible spoon up to her mouth, and she
closed her mouth around nothing.

Dying—not that she saw something I couldn't see.

4. Coda
A portion of a lower jaw with teeth
was the main relic;
if Johansson had found it, or Leakey,
either would have been ecstatic.

Airs above the Ground

—The horse stables, Vienna, 2013

1.

After telling us the meaning of pesade—
where the horse raises its forequarters, then
tucks its forelegs in—he tells us about Patton
saving Lipizzans in a mock-battle, a charade
put on by him so the Germans could save face
at the end of the war, surrender to his men,
and turn over stock spared from Allied bombing.
Patton competed in the Olympics, equestrian
events, all involving classical dressage;
he'd been alerted about the mares' location,
with some stallions, at St. Martins. By then
my father was stateside in a ward—his bandage,
a headset at his temples, wet with a sponge.

2.

"In the capriole, the horse, from a raised position,
jumps, and then it kicks out with its hind legs
while in the air. This maneuver, if failed, often
results in such injury to the animal that it begs
to be put down immediately; if successful,
the animal will be introduced to the mezair,
where the horse rears up to strike with its forelegs
as if an enemy were in front, as with the pesade,
the enemy were behind"—our guide talks; I listen.
"A horse lowering itself to ground is called the piaffe.
Patton believed that he had mastered them all."
My father's buried in Bay Pines Veterans Cemetery, Florida.
He received convulsive electro-shock for a decade.

Ghosts from the Home Front at the Café Central

—Vienna, 2013

I knew a woman beaten to a pulp.
With apologies to Roethke, when I think
of bones, I think of them over a sink
washing blood from a recently broken lip;

or when I think of how a body swayed
and moved to its own kind of music,
I'm really thinking of a zipper and fabric
being ripped apart and the sound that made;

and when I think of how I and others make light
of Trotsky and Stalin and Hitler dining here,
I have to remind myself that the brats and beer
I've enjoyed on this vacation are a birthright

given me from him who returned from war
after a darkness had invaded every cell and fiber.

Biographical Note

Stephen Gibson is the author of seven other poetry collections: *Paradise* (University of Arkansas finalist selection), *Frescoes* (Lost Horse Press book prize), *Masaccio's Expulsion* (MARGIE/Intuit House book prize), *Rorschach Art* (Red Hen Press), *The Garden of Earthly Delights Book of Ghazals* (Texas Review Press), *Self-Portrait in a Door-Length Mirror* (2017 Miller Williams Prize Winner, University of Arkansas Press, selected by Billy Collins), and *Frida Kahlo in Fort Lauderdale* (finalist, Able Muse Book Prize, forthcoming later this year). His finalist short story collection, *The Persistence of Memory*, is from Stephen F. Austin State University Press.

CPSIA information can be obtained
at www.ICGtesting.com
Printed in the USA
JSHW030329140721
16893JS00001B/63